"a tick of a time-piece
rekindled, relighted;
soul does not cease.
will we be reunited?"

~ Theodor Meron

(excerpt from 'So Little Time Is Left' pg. 26)

POEMS ON BEING, ON LOVE AND ON GRIEF

Theodor Meron

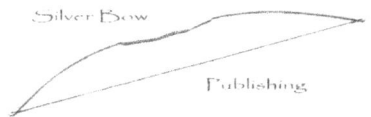

Box 5 – 720 – 6th Street,
New Westminster, BC
V3C 3C5   CANADA

Title: Poems On Being, On Love and Grief
Author: Theodor Meron
Cover Photo: by Theodor Meron
Layout/Design: Candice James
ISBN: 9781774033838 (print)
ISBN: 9781774033845 (ebk)

All rights reserved including the right to reproduce or translate this book or any portions thereof, in any form except for the use of short passages for review purposes, no part of this book may be reproduced, in part or in whole, or transmitted in any form or by any means, electronically or mechanically, including photocopying, recording, or any information or storage retrieval system without prior permission in writing from the publisher or a license from the Canadian Copyright Collective Agency (Access Copyright)
© Silver Bow Publishing 2025

Library and Archives Canada Cataloguing in Publication Title: Poems on being, on love and on grief / Theodor Meron. Names: Meron, Theodor, 1930- author. Identifiers: Canadiana (print) 2025026398X | Canadiana (ebook) 20250265737 | ISBN 9781774033838 (softcover) | ISBN 9781774033845 (Kindle) Subjects: LCGFT: Poetry. Classification: LCC PS3613.E76 P64 2025 | DDC 811/.6—dc23

In the memory of Monique,
the Love of my life.

**She whispers, *'do not cry'*
and kisses me goodbye.**

(excerpt pg. 58)

Table of Contents

In the Gardens of Villa Serbelloni / 11
In the Fiesta of San Giovanni / 13
Existential Questions / 14
The Spark / 16
Do not chase after ghosts / 17
He was a lonely boy / 18
Shipwrecked / 19
At the Western Wall / 20
A naïve answer / 23
Agenda Full / 24
Charmed Life / 25
So little time is left / 26
Fear / 27
A bird / 28
How could it happen? / 29
Rain in vain / 31
You touched me so / 32
Salvation / 33
I feel guilty / 34
December in Easthampton / 35
By the fireplace / 36
Memories / 37
Lake Leman, a dream / 38
You will find me out / 39
Are you for real? / 40
A foreboding of doom / 41
Will Jericho's Wall's? / 42
You chase the doom away / 43
Elvira / 44
I wish you a happy year / 46
Parting / 47
Time is passing / 48
Even from a distance / 50
So tired / 51
I long for you / 52
I stopped running / 53
Now that we are married / 54

Do not leave me / 55
A complaint / 56
In the Old Village Cemetery / 57
Just for an instant / 58
And now that you are gone /59
Envy / 60

Author Profile / 61

poems

*on being,
on love
and on grief*

In the Gardens of Villa Serbelloni

The summer air hangs still,
heavy, immobile. Nil
interrupts this dreamy silence
sharpened only by the dalliance
of birds, which fills the void.

Distant church bells
softly tell tales,
without tearing the fragile fabric
unmeasurable by any yardstick
of beauty or emotion.
and beyond any notion
of the banal and the ordinary
and yet, alas, so very transitory.

The trees move at the wind's direction.
The lake suggests a soft reflection
of the mountains' birth and glory.
Or is it just creation's story?
Or my imagination?
An optical illusion?
A lazy day's confusion?
Or the fragrance of tranquility
unattainable in reality.

The rugged peak
my eyes now seek
was, in the wind,
earlier today,
overbearing and menacing,
in the dawn's rays;
now, in the fog,
only a silhouette.

It quickly blends
with the pale sky,
tests my imagination

and my sight
as if it were already night.

I still recognize subtle profiles
of mountain crests
villages on the rocks nest.

A sailboat crawls in the evening mist.
My God, how I shall miss all this!

A ferryboat moors
at the Bellagio dock;
the twilight sets in and
I can't stop the clock.

In the Fiesta of San Giovanni, in San Giovanni, da Bellagio

The local band played Adagio.
In the dark we danced
breathless, entranced,
to a nostalgic and faded waltz.

The moored boats gently rolled.
The crowd was robust.
The music became fast.
A white-haired man danced
with his aging daughter.
A hundred candles flickered in the water.

A tired farmer, with bent figure,
waltzed with surprising vigor.
Children gyrated lightly
and their parents moved sprightly.

Fireworks lit the sky.
The ambiance made me high.
Time stopped for a bit,
then the sound and light quit.

There was only now...
                      only now.

Existential Questions

Are we erratic actors in a theatre of the absurd?
Or robots moving in predetermined orbits
devoid of suspense?

Are we controlled by blind fate?
Governed by our birth, its place and date?
Why are some of us happier than others?
For what do we owe thanks to our fathers?
Are we guided by stars in their firmaments?
By our parents' deeds and testaments?
Or by our own sins and our own omissions.
Are we in the throes of struggling transitions
that lead to a world of gentle ease
in which there is a lasting peace.
Teeming with fairness and humaneness.
A world without wars, cruelties or meanness.
Or are we in transit to eternal oblivion
which awaits the human quadrillion.

What is the secret of the cycles
for which even confident disciples
of science do not have explanations?
What is the depth of love's dispensations
How does one calculate the vast years
alternating with love, fears and tears?
In the ebb and flow of tides of desire,
some souls are extinguished and some set afire.
Is that where joy holds hands with exhilaration?
Or are they displaced by disgrace and dejection?

Do heavy clouds of existential sorrow,
sometimes give way, in the wake of tomorrow?
And what of brief clearings of intense rays?
It's a never-ending cosmic quest for survival—
The struggle for life since humans' arrival.

The human condition's a constant reminder.
Are we here by the grace of a grand designer?

A hug, a squeeze, a gentle kiss
and it all comes down to this:

Cycles of ease and stress.
A rhythm of life and death.

The Spark

In love there is a fragile flame.
Alas I do not know the name
and there is trust, warmth and desire
as long as love survives the fire.

There is a magic wand
that fills our deepest want.
There is a secret spark
lighting up the dark
enigma of the human soul
locked in a mysterious role.

But if this flame has become smothered
an ember may still be recovered.
The smallest spark can burst to flame
In the name of love's slick game.

Please, do not cry, my dear.
I'm still here and very near.

But even if the spark should die
and love should breathe its final sigh
we shall always be the same:
In poetry we will remain.

Do not chase after ghosts

Try not to recreate days lost and bygone
or attempt to resurrect yesterday's dawn.
The past should be viewed through a fine mist,
through soft moonbeams and skies star-kissed.

Run not after ghosts.
Do not try to grasp their essence.
They will rob you of the present.

Don't force a memory to revive.
The past is dead and you're alive.
Your expectations would fall flat,
like the rabbit trapped inside the hat.

Do not chase after ghosts.
They always make poor hosts.

He was a lonely boy

He was a lonely boy,
who grew up without a toy.
He was kept out of sight,
hidden from the light

He grew up with no mother to soothe
the anxieties of a young boy's youth.
He was without a friend, without a school
All alone in an empty room.

All alone, always alone.

But one thing he had in abundance
to help him through the silence
was his camaraderie with fantasy
allowing escapes from reality
to visit a beautiful imaginary world
where nature's bounties were unfurled
in fields, forests and rolling oceans
where he could freely follow all his notions.
Where he had no fear or need to be timid.
Where his dreams had no limit.
Where all his prayers had no bounds
as he listened to the sounds..

Shipwrecked

Two shipwrecked souls
in a stormy ocean
are swaying close
in constant motion.

Their arms are bruised,
all their strength used;
but now their hands touch
and the feeling is such
that closer together
now, they are drawn
and they drown in each other
in love's bittersweet dawn.

At the Western Wall

At the Western Wall, the place of truth,
with you in the women's section;
a beloved stranger in the
land of Jews.

Damp was the air. Wet was the ground.
Chilling rain. Wind's howling sound.

It was here Jews were bled
in the burning Temple turned red
by the Romans who trod upon
their lifeless bodies at dawn,
near these Herodian stones
now a graveyard of bones.

It still feels today so strangely awry.
I can almost hear their hapless ghosts cry.

There today I prayed to God
in the hazy catch of winter's fog
in the pull of yesterday's synagogue,
to spare the pain and suffering
from people who are wondering
whether I have abandoned them.

And if I'm sane I'll start again.

A man my age, today,
hair receding and temples gray,
sight is fading and eyes are weak;
but my voice is strong and so I speak,
praying for those who still love me
safe passage in life's stormy sea;
and for those that love me no longer
may they be happy and keep growing stronger.
And above all... yes dear God... above all,
if pain comes to them may it be small.

A man my age, at the Western Wall
not strong, not tall but giving his all,
bending his head and praying to God
sending him a heartfelt thought
trying to find a way to start again
in the hold of His love and the warm winter rain.

At the Western Wall I bare my soul,
pray for peace and warmth from the cold,
and health and ease from heaven above.
And most of all I pray for our Love
that our fate be blessed in our aging years
and our tribulations with very few tears.

I pray for the future of all generations.
May they have happiness and exultations.
May the young be our joy and consolation
in years of declining strength and depreciation.

>May we not be too weak
>for companionship
>and may we be blessed
>with true friendship.
>Please give the young
>protection and shelter
>from humanity's vile
>and evil temper.

May they not be orphaned young
keep them safe and protected
until they can shine and stand on their own
like a bright rising sun at dawn

May they be blessed by goodness,
excellent health as they strive
and endowed with outstanding fitness
that they may thrive and survive.

I did have my doubts
at the Western Wall.
I saw the clouds gathering
and knew rain must fall.

I prayed in solitude
and sacred silence
for God's mercy and His
benevolent guidance.

A naïve answer

To the mystery of our fate,
for me, at any rate,
the answer is certain and not new.
In the end we all get our due.

So, sew your seeds with love and care.
Wins only count if you play fair.

Our open wounds need not go untreated
if we strive with verve to be undefeated.
If you're vigilant you'll see the signs
and know the truth of fate's designs.

We must always strive to be our best;
and at the ready for all life's tests.
Mercy and anger walk hand in hand
but know for certain that life can be grand.

Though many questions may remain,
our search for them is not in vain;
but who can explain
the reason for little children's pain?

Agenda Full

There are so many things I want to do;
but only with you ... only with you.
So many sights to take in and explore
fantasies to transform and so much more.
Let us share our coveted dreams
and indulge together our secret whims.

We were not born for pantomime.
Though together we have so little time;
but here in love's spin of push and pull
we know we've been blessed. Agenda full.

Charmed Life

I hope I do not sin when I say,
that with you near me, every day
I live a charmed life:
without strife,
without tension,
or negation,
without clouds,
and without doubts.

Have I told you that you're my paradise?
I can see heaven in your bright eyes.
You'll have no cause to doubt my love.
I swear this to all the gods above.

I've lived a charmed life it's true.
And it's all because of you.

All because of you.

So little time is left

So little time is left
and soon you'll take my leave;
but don't decry this theft
of our sublime happiness.
There is no need to grieve.

As love's embers burn
happiness will return.
Serenity and peace
will come with ease.
Without a doubt
all fear wiped out.

And what shall survive
to surely thrive?
Only affection
Without any question.

A tick of a time piece
rekindled, relighted;
Soul does not cease
will we be reunited?

Our last dance of love,
by bright stars above,
will last forever
in sunshine and rain
where we will be one
and part — never again.

Fear

Will you one day
be swayed
by another male
whom you desire more
than you loved me yore?

How can I know
that the answer is no?

Please make it so.
Whisper soft and low
and kiss me as you answer *'no.'*

A bird

Like a bird that has been hurt,
afraid to try
again to fly

Don't fear, my Love.
Your fate was tough
but you will have it whipped.
Your wings have not been clipped.
You will soar and fly again
toward the sun from out the rain.

I pray to God
that I should not
add to your pain
in earnest or vain.

By your sadness touched,
so much.

How could it happen?

I was too scarred to think of love
too wounded to desire
and although my armour was tough
only in my dreams dared I aspire.

Feeling old
for the world,
and certain of rejection
I refused all affection.

My hedges were careful
my bets were small
I set strict limits
to cushion a fall

Limited liability I made sure I had
like a finely structured corporation;
and safe was the path of the life I led
like a pious monk's first incarnation.

Loner in a crowd
conscious of my route
everything was wistful.
Nothing was blissful.

Then you came, out of the blue,
and you became wonderful You.

I think in a haze.
I walk in a daze.
I'm in love with a capital "L."
What I feel I cannot tell.

Was it your shy smiles?
Your soft female wiles?
Your remoteness from rile?
Your humility?

your integrity?
or your ability
to be just yourself, so truthful
your manner so innocent and youthful.

Now I dream again
I walk a wholly new terrain:
the mountains of the world,
the valleys of the cross,
forests ever green,
beaches clean, pristine,
with you by my side
riding love's high tide.

With you, the sky is the limit,
although I'm anxious and timid.
With my eye fixed on the goal
I play the whole bankroll
to conquer happiness
and vanquish emptiness.

Rain in vain

Rain
in vain.

Snow
in tow.

Freeze
no tease.

Fog
no yoke.

Clouds
no match.

With you around
It's serene and sound.
Harsh elements
are drowned.

You touched me so

You touched me so
and I don't know
is my pain
in vain?

No, it is true
because it's you.

Salvation

Like fresh air
an auspicious year.
Not just a temptation
but a salvation;

and salvation
is redemption.

I feel guilty

I feel guilty
for nothing in particular
and for everything;
but in the singular.

Because I love you so
to others I say no.
From you I've taken so much.
Taken, without giving such.

I feel responsible for humanity
who are mired in adversity.
It simply is not fair
to be so happy, yet ... I dare.

December in Easthampton

The ocean
in constant motion.
The waves
that no one tames.

The seagulls in their flight.
There is no one in sight.
The sand is white and wet.
Your cap, my Love, is red.

The air is clear.
Our only tear
is of happiness.
Our hearts' in readiness
to stop the clock
at the deserted dock.

By the fireplace

We look at the fire.
No need for a wire
to transmit our emotion.
Music carries our notion
of love, eternal.
No force, external,
can touch our truth
stronger than youth.

The burning logs —
our dreamy thoughts

Memories

Stealthily, through the crack, old memories enter
and go straight for my vulnerable nerve center.
They are bittersweet or mostly bitter-ache.
Thoughts that should lay dormant, suddenly awake.
Brittle chips fall from the soul and they snap and break
to clean dust away, and revive the past,
to put back together the pieces that crashed
persons, events, and forgotten terms
expose unhealed wounds and loose old germs.
to bite and inflict guilt, doubts and pain.
Misspent memories pour forth like hard rain.

Finally, my senses of self-preservation
chase them away, and seek expiation;
but I know that one day somewhere down the road
they will come back again and they'll unload
troubling memories from the past, the West and the East.
Uninvited guests when I desire them least.

Lake Leman, a dream

On Lake Leman, we sail
under the veil.

Your frail figure,
with surprising vigour,
steers our boat
on our high road.

You touch me so
my inner sanctums raw
and, so together, now we row.

You will find me out

One day
you will find me out
with no redeeming ray
and you will fade away.

And that day —
I will be no more.

Are you for real?

Are you for real?
And will you stay?
or be an illusion
which goes away, a trek
that leaves behind a broken wreck?

Like a child now, I pray
each night and every day
that you should love Me too
as deeply as I love You.

A foreboding of doom

Fear takes over tonight.
Nothing seems to be right.
It's dark in the room.
A foreboding of doom.
A steady drizzling rain
and you are far away.

Anxieties and doubts.
Wind's howling sounds
turn me inside out;
turn me upside down
and I'm about to drown.

God give me love and peace
without pain; and with ease.

Will Jericho's Walls?

Will Jericho's walls
come down on my happiness?
Is the bell which tolls
a signal of my loneliness?

Will the envious distort
our perfect rapport?
Will our love last
or be covered by dust?

The gathering storm
threatens our love, so warm.

Shall we overcome animosity,
be saved by our felicity
or, doomed for mediocrity,
go down in obscurity?

You chase the doom away

You chase the doom away.
You shine the edge of day.
Your presence in the room
repels the gloom and doom,
drives away all fears
and quickly dries my tears.

Your tender loving voice:
drowns all the ugly noise,
kills all the nagging doubts,
disperses the storm clouds,
and always reassures me
that even in a rough sea
our Love will always be
the epitome of victory.

Elvira

My window is by the precipice
looking into the guilty abyss
and the pained eyes of Dona Elvira.
This is not a cinema
but life with all its cruelty
which is not a novelty
I know I inflicted it.
And it makes my soul feel sick
when I think of her hellish confusion
and her hoping it was just an illusion;
but it was a reality
of love lost a certainty
an end to a dream she had
where evidence of love lay dead.
And how she cried
as her dream died.
Alas it was me who made her cry
and all I could conjure up was a sigh.

The light grew bright as it neared
Then suddenly you appeared.
I knew without hesitation
this was not just a temptation
but a Love that comes once in a lifetime
not just an affair which occurs time to time.

I knew I could not just let you pass
but had to hold onto you and hold you fast
I dumped overboard all the rest
because this was the final test
and I had no chance to have a choice.
Sometimes I still imagine the noise
of her moaning in sorrow and sadly crying
and still my conscience continues sighing.
It's such a shame that our happiness
had to cause her such emptiness.

May she forget me forever and soon.
May she find true love under a new moon.

One day let her find
happiness with another.
Someone to embrace her heart
and forever love her.

Dona Elvira I wish you love's zest
The top of the mark ...
The best of the best!

I wish you a happy year

I wish you a happy year
days passing without a tear;
shelter from chilling rain,
a year without pain.

Joy's clarion call.
God's angels standing tall.
May God be good to you
and may our Love be true.

May obstacles vanish.
Affection be cherished.
May God give you good health
and spiritual wealth.
May He give you long life
full of hope and lovelight.
Love in great density
laced with immensity.
A year without tension.
Of rancor, no mention.
Safe in a circle of trust
may our Love repel all rust.

And so, my dear
from far, yet so near,
I wish you a good rest
And this year be the best.

Parting

And once again we part in pain.
the plane takes off, no rain,
brilliant sunshine this time.

Last kiss, audible sighs.
Declarations and vows.
Deep down a slow sadness.
A memory of tenderness.
The disappearing ground.
The engine's soothing sound.

Sweet secrets bring a smile
and warm our hearts awhile.

All fears and doubts are gone.
Now the count-down is on
to our reunion in 50 days.
Short, but so long in so many ways.

May they pass fast like a summer wind's gust
before our emotions can gather dust.

Time is passing

Now, many a day
you have been far away
and I have longed for your touch
so very much.

I've been counting days
without sun's rays
yet I feel so sure
of your soul so pure.

Since you are with me in spirit
it takes no great merit
to survive, and to stay alive
floating into your Love, I dive.

I know that you
dream of me too.

Our separation:
a sad aberration.
a temporary intrusion.
a momentary occlusion.

The days are passing fast.
The die of love is cast
to revive our emotion,
sail again on love's ocean.

For many a day
you've been far away.
I've longed for your touch
so very much.

You're here
my dear.

You kiss me softly
and whisper hush.

I love you, my sweet,
so very much.

Even from a distance

It is a miracle!
Even from a distance
you tackle
my foul mood.
When I am mean and rude
the thought of your touch
does so much
to soothe my body and soul.
Please keep this role
on a permanent contract
and let there be no distance in our contact.

So tired

I am tired and low.
Events have me in tow.
I can do nothing right.
I can't control my life.

No strength left to do.
No drive to renew.

leave me alone and let me sleep
in hibernation long and deep.

I long for you

I long for you
and for the day when I am due.
I wish it would arrive
for I am only half alive
waiting to wed my bride
on an afternoon of blessed light.

The dawn of days
of love and grace
in your tender embrace.

I see them shining,
aglow, on your radiant face.

I stopped running

Life has been cruel.
An endless duel
with people and events,
with atmospheres dense
and everything tense.

Now I can stop running
and even sighing.

I have arrived.
My home I've found.

Now that we are married

And now, that we have tarried
with each other and we've married
and promised to love and to cherish
our bond is stronger and won't perish.
We'll love each other past forever
and nothing will lessen or ever sever
the intensity and warmth of our emotion
of trust and affection, on our private ocean.

Our wedding was not a formality
nor just a legal necessity;
but something we truly wanted
to become one and be anointed
with a vow and a sacrament
to protect us from detriment.
Our union of Love will last and thrive
as long as we are both alive.

I thank you, Darling, for being my wife:
my alter ego, my entire life.

Do not leave me

Oh, please do not leave me
to where I cannot see.
I hold your hand, no longer warm;
no help, to my heart, torn.

No smile on your face.
No semblance of embrace
and only immense pain.

A complaint

Why do you choose the best
your afflictions to test?

Did you aim at her eyes
as her first sacrifice
to make her see all black
and be a living wreck?

Could you not heal her sore
or wait a little more?

In your tenacity
And pitiless alacrity
you took her without agony;
Left me solitude, grief and misery.

In the Old Village Cemetery

Weeds and decaying leaves.
Cypress and olive trees.
Neglected, crumbling walls.
A resting place for souls.
Graves all alone.
Grief made my heart stone.
Silence of a small village.
A lazy, sleepy image.
Family mausoleum.
I will not sing te Deum.

No one at all in sight.
Spider webs all 'round tonight.
I used to come and pray
(and thank your parents for the gift)
of you one blessed day.
Now I pray for your serenity
complaining to God for this fatality
of taking you from me.
Yesterday in the open pine coffin
I kissed your cold lips I could still see.
Now I kiss your sealed coffin
before it's laid down there
in your family's grave.
One day my coffin too
will lie there with you.

Our bones resting together
in our final embrace
in sunny weather.

                        Kyrie Eleison

Just for an instant

Send her on a furlough
so, she can fly below
just for an instant
all this distance.
Be it in a dream
transported by a beam
let her come as she was
without her angels' host
and without her halo
just with her own glow
telling me she loves me so;
and she can see me still
and feel my body's chill.

She whispers, *'do not cry'*
and kisses me goodbye.

And now that you are gone

Now you have crossed the Rubicon
from the land of the living.
For taking you away,
to God, there's no forgiving.

You are gone to the space of the dead,
and the darkness of dread.
To keep me living, I make no plea.
For to die, I would be free.
My fear dissipates in time's tide
as I climb the steps to be by your side.

And I pray for the dawn
when you're no longer gone;
I'll climb through heaven's hole.
Will I find your blessed soul?

Envy

I envy couples holding hands
wandering streets together making plans
eyes aglow, radiating love
fitting each other like a glove.

I recall us walking ... you half-blind
clutching my hand, your world undefined.

Now it is I, seeking your hand
as all alone I stand
in the unkind, hostile air,
so cold without you there.

A loving couple passes by.
I feel a tear fill in my eye
and then for a minute or two
I'm lost in longing for you

But alas your soul has flown.
I'm standing here alone.

As the hourglass drains its sands
I envy couples holding hands.

THEODOR MERON CMG.

Theodor Meron, born in Poland in 1930, has been a Judge and, between March 2012 and January 2019, was the President of the International Residual Mechanism for Criminal Tribunals (Mechanism). He was also the President of the Appeals Chambers of the International Criminal Tribunal for the former Yugoslavia (ICTY) and the International Criminal Tribunal for Rwanda (ICTR). He served four terms as President of the ICTY and three terms as President of the Mechanism, a unique record in the international judiciary.

A leading scholar of international humanitarian law, human rights, and international criminal law, Judge Meron is the author of twelve books, mostly on international law and two on chivalry in Shakespeare, one of which received the best book award from the American Society of International Law, and more than a hundred articles, including some of the books and articles that helped build the legal foundations for international criminal tribunals. His most recent book is Standing up for Justice (OUP 2021).

He has taught at NYU Law School, Harvard, Geneva, and Oxford. His interviews and profiles appeared in Atlantic monthly, Lines Magazine, Foreign Policy, The Prospect Magazine, Der Spiegel and Le Monde, among others.

He is a member of the Institute of International Law and of the Council on Foreign Relations, a Fellow of the American Academy of Arts and Sciences, and the recipient of numerous awards, honors, and medals, such as the Hudson Medal (ASIL) (the highest distinction of ASIL) and the Haskins Prize (ACLS),

Officer of the French Legion of Honour, Grand Officer of the French National Order of Merit, Officer of the Order of Merit of Poland and Companion of the Most Distinguished Order of St. Michael and St. George of the United Kingdom and Honorary Citizen of Kalisz. A past honorary President of the American Society of International Law, past Editor-in-Chief of the American

Journal of International Law, and past Visiting Fellow of All Souls College, Oxford, he is Charles L. Denison Professor of Law Emeritus at NYU Law School and, since 2014, a Visiting Professor of Law at Oxford University.

He is a Visiting Fellow at Mansfield College, an Academic Associate of Oxford Bonavero Human Rights Institute, and an Honorary Fellow at Trinity College. He is a renowned judge, scholar, and author. He received doctorates in Honoris Causa from the University of Warsaw and Calisia.

He was special adviser to the Prosecutor of the International Criminal Court (2022-2025). As child and teenager, he survived the Holocaust in ghettos and a labor camp. He was later smuggled out of Communist Poland and studied law at the Universities of Jerusalem, Harvard, and Cambridge.

He has had distinguished and varied careers as a diplomat at the rank of Ambassador, Legal Adviser to the Foreign Ministry of Israel, Counsellor on International Law to the US State Department, an Ambassador to Canada, and President of UN War Crimes Tribunals, as a leading professor of law, and now as a visiting professor of law in Oxford and Honorary Fellow of Trinity College. He has written landmark decisions on genocide, crimes against humanity, and war crimes.

As a legal adviser in Israel, he authored a famous opinion in 1967 declaring the illegality of settlements in the West Bank. He is considered one of the world's authorities on international justice. His memoir (A Thousand Miracles: from surviving the Holocaust to Judging Genocide) will be published by Hurst Publications in London. One of his poems was published by Oxford Review of Books in May 2025.

www.ingramcontent.com/pod-product-compliance
Lightning Source LLC
Chambersburg PA
CBHW071254070526
44583CB00017B/2469